Using Wind
to Make Electricity

Here comes the wind.

3

Woosh!

Look at the leaves.

Look at the umbrella.

Look at this.

This will go round

and round in the wind.

The wind will make electricity.

11

The electricity will make my computer go.

The electricity will make my **light** go.

15

Glossary

 light

 pinwheel